Did ...

RED...

A MISCELLANY

Compiled by Julia Skinner
With particular reference to the work of Julie Royle

THE FRANCIS FRITH COLLECTION

www.francisfrith.com

Based on a book first published in the United Kingdom in 2006 by The Francis Frith Collection®

Hardback edition published in 2008 ISBN 978-1-84589-397-2

British Library Cataloguing in Publication Data

Did You Know? Redditch - A Miscellany
Compiled by Julia Skinner
With particular reference to the work of Julie Royle

The Francis Frith Collection
Frith's Barn, Teffont,
Salisbury, Wiltshire SP3 5QP
Tel: +44 (0) 1722 716 376
Email: info@francisfrith.co.uk
www.francisfrith.com

Printed and bound in Singapore

Front Cover: **REDDITCH, THE POST OFFICE, EVESHAM STREET c1955** R84037ap

The colour-tinting is for illustrative purposes only, and is not intended to be historically accurate

AS WITH ANY HISTORICAL DATABASE, THE FRANCIS FRITH ARCHIVE IS CONSTANTLY BEING
CORRECTED AND IMPROVED, AND THE PUBLISHERS WOULD WELCOME INFORMATION ON
OMISSIONS OR INACCURACIES

CONTENTS

INTRODUCTION

Redditch is located in the north-east corner of Worcestershire, on the Warwickshire border sixteen miles south of Birmingham. Redditch's population growth was rapid in the 19th century. From the 1840s onwards the town became increasingly built up, and in 1894 it was made an Urban District. This rapid expansion during the 19th century was followed by slower but steady growth throughout the 20th century. Between 1929 and 1933 Ipsley, Feckenham, Crabbs Cross, Astwood Bank and parts of Alvechurch and Webheath were taken into Redditch. New housing estates were built at Batchley, Mayfields, Abbeydale and Studley Road.

In 1964 the population of Redditch was around 32,000, and the town was poised on the brink of a new era - in that year it was designated a New Town to house Birmingham overspill and to alleviate overcrowding in the West Midlands conurbation; Redditch began a period of enormous change, the most dramatic in the town's history. By the time the Redditch Development Corporation was wound down in 1985 the population had doubled in size and thousands of new homes had been built, together with millions of square feet of industrial and office space. A new road network had been imposed, and the Victorian town centre had been redeveloped to include a huge shopping mall, the Kingfisher Shopping Centre, of dubious 1970s and 1980s architectural merit. The town was planned as a series of 'neighbourhoods', each with about 10,000 people, in which houses were grouped around a local centre providing essential services, while industrial areas, schools and other facilities were built nearby. The design of Redditch's New Town development was intended to create a feeling of wide open spaces with landscaped housing estates integrated into the environment. Opinions differ as to how successfully this was achieved, but there is certainly plenty

of green space. The massive Arrow Park runs through the heart of the borough, incorporating woods, water meadows, a large lake with sports and leisure facilities, and a fair amount of wildlife too.

There was much opposition to the New Town development, and many local people old enough to remember Redditch as it was will never be reconciled to what has happened. Others, especially some of those who moved into the area from the West Midlands conurbation, think it a fine place in which to live and work. Redditch is now the second largest town in Worcestershire, having overtaken old-established market centres such as Bromsgrove, Kidderminster and Evesham.

WOOLWORTH'S, THE MARKET PLACE c1960 R84044a

LOCAL WORDS AND PHRASES

'Tadgers' - a local name for policemen.

'Peckers' - a local name for policemen's helmets.

'Kingfisher' - a local name for a shoplifter.

'Swing' - a local name for a roundabout, as in the phrase **'swings and roundabouts'**.

'Twitters' - the name for small pieces of broken metal which got into the eyes of needle pointers.

A glimpse of life in Redditch in the mid 19th century is found in the following rhyme, written in 1840, which is quoted in 'Needlemaking' by John G Rollins (Shire Publications, 1981):

> In hurden* aprons and paper caps
> The scourers looked such funny chaps.
> Blue-pointers dressed like other men
> For they were thought quite gentlemen.
> What wicked men the pointers were
> To drink and curse and fight and swear -
> A short and merry life they'd lead
> And of the future take no heed.
> Hard times for those who'd work
> Twelve hours a day, one couldn't shirk.
> The bell was rung, and you must hear
> Or the 'sack' you'd get first pay day near.
> Saturdays brought them no enjoyment
> They stayed till six at their employment.
> Boys and girls eight, nine and ten
> Toed the mark with women and men.
> Village stampers brought their pockets
> Hung in wallets behind their jackets.
> With ninety thousand on heel and toe
> 'Twas a hard walk from Crowder's Row**

* 'hurden' was a type of coarse linen.   ** Crowder's Row was in Crabbs Cross. The blue-pointers mentioned in line 3 made the points of the needles, and were considered to be of higher standing than other workers as they commanded high wages for their skills (see also page 21). The 'ninety thousand' of line 19 probably refers to the number of needles that had been made, and which were being carried to a delivery point.

HAUNTED REDDITCH

The website www.geocities.com/ghostsofredditch features a fascinating selection of ghost stories from the Redditch area - there are more than you might think!

The Birmingham Evening Mail on 16 February 2001 reported a ghost story linked with the Brockhill Women's Prison near Redditch. Prisoners had reported seeing a ghost in the shape of a monk apparently passing through solid walls, and the story was supported by some members of staff who admitted to feeling particularly uneasy on nightshifts. The prison was built in 1965 in the former grounds of Hewell Grange, a manor owned by the Earl of Plymouth; the Hewell Grange estate had links with Bordesley Abbey, which may be the reason for the roaming spectre.

A ghost known as 'Old Friendly Tom' is reported on the Ghosts of Redditch website as haunting a house in Lakeside in the 1980s. 'Tom' is believed to have lived in the house in the 1950s or 1960s. The ghost, which was assumed to be responsible for moving a plant pot around the house, was seen by the man of the house several times and his grandchildren were also frightened by a shadowy figure walking around a room in the house.

The Forge Mill Needle Museum at Needle Mill Lane, Riverside is said to be haunted by several ghosts, one of which may be the shade of a needle-pointer called Edward Matthews, who was killed in an accident in 1816 when the pointing stone shattered. A piece of the stone which killed him was inscribed and built into the wall of the East Wing of the building, and can still be seen. The ghost of the man who set the fragment of stone which killed Edward Matthews in the wall is also supposed to haunt the building, as he himself was killed when he fell from the ladder whilst putting it in place.

Trinity High School in Easemore Road is believed to be haunted by a ghost which may be the shade of the first headmaster of the original school on this site. Every year, on 17 May, the ghost is said to walk along the top corridor under the bell house.

REDDITCH MISCELLANY

A New Town Redditch may be, but it is not so very new, although Redditch did develop later than other Worcestershire towns. The first recorded mention of a settlement on the site of the present-day Redditch town centre dates from the founding of Bordesley Abbey by Cistercian monks in 1138. The monks owned huge estates on which they raised sheep, and they soon grew rich from the wool trade. They were skilled engineers: they diverted the River Arrow, built an extensive drainage system, created fish ponds and harnessed water power to drive a corn mill and two other mills used for industrial purposes. Exactly when a lay settlement began to develop alongside the abbey is unclear, but the monks would have required a workforce and we know that by 1248 a hamlet called Rededitch or Red-dyche was in existence.

St Stephen's Church (see photograph R84001, opposite) stands on Church Green, the area around which people first settled when they moved from Bordesley after the abbey there was dissolved in the 16th century. Church Green is still, in many ways, the focal point of the redeveloped town. In 1855 St Stephen's replaced the Chapel on the Green, built in 1805 to replace the ancient chapel at Bordesley. The architect was Henry Woodyer of Guildford, but his rather uninspiring Decorated-style church was substantially restored and extended in 1893-94 by Temple Moore. The local sandstone is not particularly durable, and St Stephen's has needed more than one restoration in the course of its relatively short life. On one such occasion, in 1905-06, it is said that the town librarian, Mr Lewis, took advantage of the scaffolding to climb to the top of the spire. Dragging a cumbersome plate camera with him, he took four photographs, looking north, south, east and west.

ST STEPHEN'S CHURCH
c1950 R84001

Did You Know?
REDDITCH
A MISCELLANY

CHURCH GREEN c1950 R84016

Many of the trees on Church Green were planted in the 1850s, when prosperous locals were invited to plant a tree for the hefty sum of £5 each. The building visible through the trees on Church Green in the above photograph is Smallwood Hospital, paid for by the needle-makers Edwin and William Smallwood in 1895; it still houses clinics and other medical facilities, although the town now has a modern hospital, the Alexandra Hospital, away from the town centre.

The Redditch area was traversed by many feet in ancient times - two prehistoric trackways pass through the borough, and the Roman road known as Ryknield (or Icknield) Street bypasses the town centre by a couple of miles. There is also an earthwork at Beoley which may possibly be an Iron Age fort, although there is no real evidence of any settlement at this time.

After initially flourishing, Bordesley Abbey suffered various setbacks, most notably the devastation of the Black Death in 1348. It never fully recovered, and was dissolved in 1538 during the reign of Henry VIII. The abbey was dismantled, the monks were pensioned off and most of the lay community moved to higher, drier ground where the modern town of Redditch now stands. Only the abbey's gatehouse chapel remained intact, and the people of Redditch continued to use it until 1805, when it was demolished. Since 1969 comprehensive and continuing excavations have revealed much of the floor plan of the abbey, as well as many artefacts and skeletons.

EVESHAM STREET c1950 R84008

ALCESTER STREET 1949 R84013

Most of Alcester Street was demolished in the 1960s, but the small part of it seen in this photograph survived. The building to the left of the prominent awning was Watkins' Tea Rooms at the beginning of the 20th century, and the northern gable end (not visible in this photograph) still carries the legend 'luncheon, dining, tea rooms' and also advertises accommodation for cyclists.

EVESHAM STREET 1967 R84057

ASTWOOD BANK, THE PARK c1965 A163352

Redditch's main claim to fame in history is its association with the humble needle. For many years Redditch was pre-eminent in the industry of needle manufacture, which first came to England in the late 1550s, introduced to London by Flemish immigrants. In the 1640s needle-making was becoming established in Studley and Sambourne, where it was based on the cottage system. As it flourished, it spread to other localities, reaching Alcester in 1670 and Redditch in the early 1700s. By the 1770s it was the major employer in Redditch, which was still a village at that time.

Water power was an important factor in the development of Redditch's needle-making industry, and corn mills on the River Arrow were converted into needle mills, though many of the processes were carried out in the workers' homes. It was only in the early 19th century that a steam-powered factory system was developed.

On the northern side of Arrow Park the excavated ruins of Bordesley Abbey can be seen in Abbey Meadows, and the adjacent Forge Mill Museum links Redditch's monastic origins with its industrial heritage, featuring the only surviving water-driven needle mill in the world.

The first documented needle-makers in Redditch were the Sherward brothers in the early 18th century, but more famous names include Henry Milward, and Abel Morrall, both founders of large needle-making companies.

In 1830 there was a great strike at Redditch owing to the introduction of machinery for stamping the needles, which was threatening needle-workers' jobs. Much damage was done and eight men were imprisoned. The strikers were eventually persuaded to return and learn about the new methods. However, mechanisation was still causing concern in 1840, when broadside copies of a 12-verse doggerel poem titled 'The Needle Makers Lamentation' was being sold to raise money by 'a party of needle makers from Redditch, Worcestershire, who have been thrown out of employment by the rapid improvement of machinery, as two men and three boys can do the work of 10 men'.

It is believed that in the 1850s up to 100 million needles were made every week in and around Redditch, when a staggering 90% of the world's needles were made in the area and the quality of the product was deemed second to none. Even today, there are still craftspeople the world over who will only use Redditch-made needles for their work. The raw material for needle-making was high quality steel wire, which in the Redditch area could be sourced from both nearby Birmingham and the more distant Sheffield.

In 1838 there was an outbreak of smallpox in Redditch. Young children were particularly susceptible to this disease, and William Avery in 'Old Redditch - Being an Early History of the Town From 1800 to 1850' reported that the landlord of the Horse and Jockey buried five of his children in the space of three weeks.

EVESHAM STREET c1960 R84038x

HUINS SHOES, MARKET PLACE c1955 R84027a

Photograph R84027a, above, shows Huins Shoes, which dominated the corner of Market Place for over half a century. James Huins also had shops in Evesham, Northfield and King's Norton, but the main branch was here in Redditch, along with the head office. It was advertised rather grandly as Boot Metropole.

The market at Redditch originally took place on the Green, but was confined to the south side of it after the Chapel on the Green was built in 1805. It was only then that the street now known as Market Place got its name. In 1949 the market was moved to Red Lion Street, but since then Market Place has been pedestrianised and the market is now back on two sides of the Green - Market Place and Church Green East.

In 1875 a report by the Officer of Health found that many houses in the poorer areas of Redditch, such as Edward Street and Walford Street, had pools of water in their cellars, damp walls, small rooms, and lacked both a water supply and adequate drainage. The inhabitants of such houses would have collected water from wells such as that at Pool Place, which were often contaminated. The residents of areas such as Silver Street, Hill Street and George Street had more convenient facilities of standpipes in communal courtyards, an only marginally safer arrangement. Contaminated water was one of the main causes of cholera, and Redditch was afflicted with an outbreak of cholera in 1832.

THE PARADE, CHURCH GREEN WEST c1950 R84009

Despite the diversity of the product produced by Redditch's
needle-makers, it would have been dangerous for the town to be
totally reliant on one industry. Fortunately Redditch was never
in that position, and by the early 19th century the fishing tackle

trade had also become hugely important. The manufacture of
fish hooks began in Redditch around 1770, and by 1880 Samuel
Allcock & Company was the world's largest manufacturer of
fishing tackle.

THE PARADE, CHURCH GREEN WEST c1950 R84011

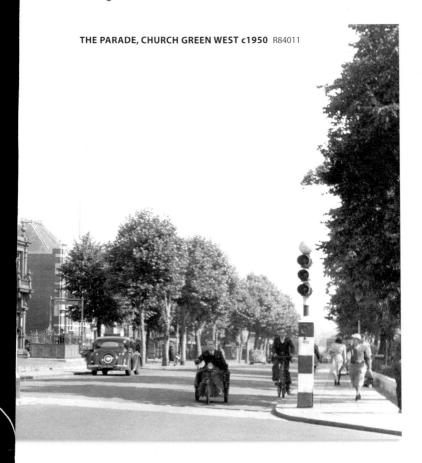

THE GARDEN OF REMEMBRANCE c1955 R84019

Before the introduction of the automatic pointing machine, around 1870, creating the points of needles was a skill done by hand. This was the best paid job in the factory, but it was also the most dangerous as slivers of metal could fly up and blind the pointer, or the grindstone itself upon which the needle-pointer was working could shatter and cause fatal injuries. Worse than these risks, however, was the danger of inhaling dust from the needles and the grindstone, and needle-pointers would often contract a crippling lung disease known as 'Pointers' Rot'. Not surprisingly, the life expectancy of a needle-pointer was no more than 35 years. E Elliot in the 1820s described the short life of a needle-pointer:

> 'There draws the grinder his laborious breath.
> There, coughing at his deadly trade he bends,
> Born to die young, he fears no man nor death,
> Scorning the future, what he earns he spends.
> Yet Abraham and Elliot both in vain
> Bid science on his cheek prolong the bloom:
> He would not live! He seems in haste to gain
> The undisturbed asylum of the tomb,
> And, old at two-and-thirty, meets his doom.'

Green-painted iron gates inscribed 'In memory of the fallen' open into Redditch's Garden of Remembrance from Plymouth Road, just around the corner from the bus station. The cenotaph does not look quite as pristine these days as it does in photograph R84019, opposite: the plaque is missing, and the niche containing the eternal flame is guarded on both sides by plastic panels.

Promotional literature published about Redditch tells us
that the existing town centre was 're-planned', an innocuous-
sounding word which, in some people's view, really means
destroyed. Photograph R84007, opposite, shows Evesham
Street in the early 1950s - almost the entire street was later
demolished to accommodate the Kingfisher Centre. Only two
or three buildings on the left of the photograph survive.

The 1875 report by the Officer of Health mentioned on page
17 counted 72 closets (toilet facilities) in use between 3,000
inhabitants; there were 700 middens in the town, of which 458 were
uncovered and considered a danger to health; and of the 43 streets
in the town, 23 had no sewers at all. Even in the new residential
area at Headless Cross (with a population of 2,000) the report found
that there were 304 houses of which 105 had no closets, and 91
households had no water supply.

The provision of safe, clean, piped water to the town in the late
19th century by the East Worcestershire Waterworks Company
was a major step forward in the health and quality of life of
the people of Redditch; in celebration of the event, Mr R S
Bartleet had a fountain erected at Church Green at his own
expense, which can still be seen today. The ornamental cast-
iron fountain, seen in photograph R84016 on page 8, was cast
at Coalbrookdale, and is an entertaining affair painted in cream
and green and featuring some life-like crested cormorants (or
shags) beneath the statue of a woman.

EVESHAM STREET c1950 R84007

THE PARADE c1950 R84017

23

THE PARADE, CHURCH GREEN WEST c1955 R84025

Another important local industry was once spring-making, which began in Redditch in the mid 19th century, its origins closely linked to the needle and fish hook trades. The most prominent manufacturer was Herbert Terry & Sons Ltd. Established in 1855, Terrys specialised at first in artificial bait, and then moved on to other precision metalware, including springs. As the cycle and car industries expanded, so did the range of goods demanded from companies such as Terrys. War was good for business too, and Terrys supplied pins for hand grenades and valve springs for the engines of Spitfires and Hurricanes; by the middle of the 20th century Terrys was producing an enormous range of products. There is still a Terry company trading in Redditch, but the involvement of the Terry family ceased in 1975; Terry of Redditch is now a hose clamp specialist and a member of the Swedish ABA group.

Photograph R84041, below, shows Alcester Street before the town centre redevelopment of the 1960s. All the foreground buildings in the photograph were destroyed. In fact, only two buildings in this scene are intact today: one is the church, and the other is the Palace Theatre (the light-coloured building behind the cyclist on the right-hand-side). The Palace Theatre has recently undergone an extensive renovation project to restore it to its former glory as an authentic Edwardian theatre, with many features of the building returned to the original design of 1913. A new town hall now stands opposite the Palace, while the foreground area has been sacrificed to the road system.

ALCESTER STREET c1955 R84041

MARKET PLACE c1955 R84040

MARKET PLACE c1950 R84012

Conflicting opinions on the merits of the modern town of Redditch are following an established tradition of like and dislike of the town in equal measure: in 1830, Walter Savage Landor (who was born at Ipsley Court) said that there never was 'an habitation more thoroughly odious - red soil, mince-pie woods, and black and greasy needleworkers', but in a poem written about 1820, John Hollis of Tardebigge declared that 'A finer village was never made' than Redditch, and for Alexander Hay Japp in 1877 it was 'a very clean and beautiful little town'.

John Noake, who travelled around Worcestershire in the 1840s and 50s, described Redditch in 1851 as an 'enterprising town with its accumulation of social comforts and advantages' with 'sparkling shops and all things betokening comfort, if not luxury'. He was told that the local needle-makers were accustomed to high wages and would scorn to work for the weekly wage of an agricultural worker (10-15 shillings), considering such a step as 'an extremity of distress'. He noted that the chapel, which could seat 1,000, filled to capacity for the Sunday service with respectable and well-behaved citizens, and was particularly impressed that 'with scarcely an exception, none of them slept during the sermon'.

There was great excitement in the town in September 1859, when Redditch was connected to the main railway network. The occasion was marked by a special excursion to Cheltenham, and a dinner at the Unicorn Hotel. Before this, passengers had to travel by road to Barnt Green and catch a train there.

EVESHAM STREET, A NEWSAGENT AND POST OFFICE c1955   R84037a

Redditch was attacked by the Luftwaffe during the Second World War on 11 December 1940, when an air raid destroyed eight houses and damaged several hundred more. The Germans were presumed to be aiming for the Alkaline Battery factory in Lodge Road, but bombs were dropped on Evesham Street, Glover Street and Orchard Street. Seven people were killed, and a further 12 were seriously injured. In line with the government censorship of the time, for security reasons, the Redditch Indicator could only report the raid in terms of an obituary saying that those who lost their lives had died 'suddenly'.

During the Second World War, Redditch was part of an area that, in the event of enemy invasion, would be the scene of activity by top-secret defence units. Members of these units were only expected to last a few weeks if called into action, and would operate from carefully camouflaged underground bases stocked with weapons and high explosives; the idea was that they would emerge at night and carry out acts of sabotage on invading forces. Redditch, together with Kidderminster and Worcester, formed part of one of Britain's inland defence systems known as 'Stop Lines', and was designated as an 'anti-tank island'. The people involved in these defence systems were sworn to secrecy, and the details of Britain's secret defence army have only recently come to light. The story of the Worcestershire area has now been told in 'The Mercian Maquis', by Bernard Lowry and Mick Wilks, published by the Logaston Press.

The town's industrial base saw considerable diversification in the 20th century. By 1964 the largest single employer was the metal manufacturing industry, followed by the engineering and spring trades, with needles and fishing tackle now some way behind, though still highly regarded in terms of quality.

Photograph R84008 on page 9 shows Evesham Street c1950. On the corner of the right-hand side is Cranmore Simmons, a family-run ironmongery firm established by Alfred Simmons in the 1920s. In photograph R84038, opposite, we can see its replacement, a Burton's store typical of 1950s building styles. This was one of the few Evesham Street buildings to survive the demolitions of the 1960s. On the left of photograph R84038, between Huins Shoes and Boots the Chemist, is E A Hodges, the long-established family-run stationers and newsagent. Hodges, which had been in Evesham Street for at least 50 years at the time of this photograph, described itself as a 'fancy repository' in early advertisements, and in 1923 the advertising slogan of the shop was 'Try Hodges First'. By the time of photograph R84057 (page 12), Hodges had become a branch of Dillons.

The Kingfisher Centre in Redditch is famous for its large mosaic panels, each of which measures 21ft x 10ft, which were designed by the famous Scottish artist and sculptor Sir Eduardo Paolozzi. The panels were created in the 1980s, and at that time they were the largest publicly commissioned works of art in the country.

Photograph R84037, opposite, shows the south end of Evesham Street in the mid 1950s, but none of this view still survives. Anybody standing today in approximately the same position as the photographer would see nothing more than a couple of dreary buildings and one of the Kingfisher Centre's multi-storey car parks. A detail of this photograph, R84037a on page 28, shows a close-up of the newsagent and post office on the left-hand side of the street - note the profusion of tobacco and cigarette advertisements!

EVESHAM STREET c1960 R84038

EVESHAM STREET c1955 R84037

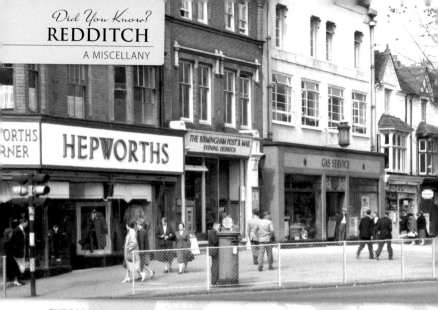

THE PARADE, CHURCH GREEN WEST c1960 R84043a

Hardly anybody refers to Church Green West as the Parade nowadays, and it is unlikely that many recall an even earlier time when it was sometimes known as the Promenade. But a few do still refer to it as Hepworths' Corner, after the shop seen on the left of photograph R84043a, above, even though Hepworths went from this site long ago.

There are several amusing stories about the Redditch needle industry, which may or may not be true. A famous one is that a foreign manufacturer once sent a tiny hypodermic needle to Redditch, claiming it as the smallest needle in the world. It was quickly returned to him with a Redditch needle threaded inside it. Another story tells how when the Japanese began their own needle-making industry they named a suburb of Tokyo as 'Redditch' so that they could legally print 'Made in Redditch' on packets of their own needles.

Ipsley was in Warwickshire when it was mentioned in the Domesday Book (1086), and only transferred to Worcestershire in 1931. It predates Redditch, but has long since been swallowed up by it. St Peter's Church, shown in photograph R84023, below, was built in 1345, probably on the site of a Saxon church. Next to it stands Ipsley Court, where the poet Walter Savage Landor (1775-1864) lived as a boy.

IPSLEY, ST PETER'S CHURCH c1955 R84023

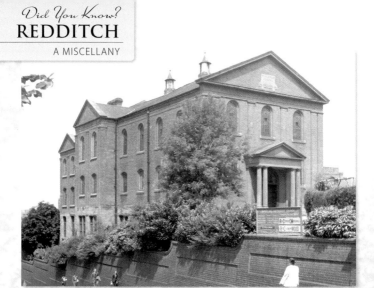

BATES HILL METHODIST CHURCH c1955 R84022

CRABBS CROSS, EVESHAM ROAD c1965 R84048

Photograph R84022, opposite, shows the imposing and quite enormous Wesleyan chapel which used to stand on Bates Hill, a testimony to the power of Methodism in 19th-century Redditch. The chapel was opened in 1843 and was extended in 1881. It was demolished in the 1980s to make way for a gas and electrical superstore.

One of the most striking things for the first-time visitor to present-day Redditch is the abundance of greenery in the area, most of which is native greenery and not foreign species introduced by inappropriate municipal planting. Only small fragments of the original woodland such as that cleared by Anglo-Saxon settlers survive, such as Pitcheroak, Foxlydiate and Oakenshaw woods, but they are authentic fragments, survivors rather than interlopers (though some non-native species have been introduced), and are bursting with bluebells in the spring. In addition to the existing woods, over 2 million trees were planted, most of them native species, as part of the massive landscaping project undertaken by the Development Corporation. Redditch also contains areas of low-lying wet meadowland, the most exciting of which is Ipsley Alders, a peat fen with rushes and sedges, which is an extremely rare habitat in the West Midlands.

Crabbs Cross mushroomed in the 19th century as rural needle-makers moved into the area to be nearer the new Redditch factories. The Star and Garter at Crabbs Cross was notorious in the 19th century for the activities which Redditch men got up to in the field behind the pub. Bull baiting, bare-knuckle boxing and cock fighting all took place there, often watched by a crowd of up to 500 men.

ASTWOOD BANK, WESTERN HILL CLOSE c1965 A163353

Redditch town centre occupies high ground near the northern end of the prehistoric Ridgeway. Astwood Bank developed in linear fashion along the Ridgeway, which is now the route of the main road to Pershore and Evesham. A wide range of architectural periods is represented in Astwood Bank, although Victorian buildings are particularly numerous. The 1960s brought a number of developments, of which that shown in photograph A163353, above, is typical. It had probably only just been completed when this photograph was taken c1965 - the gardens are obviously newly planted.

The Church of St Matthias and St George at Astwood Bank was built in 1884 and enlarged in 1911, with the works carried out by Huxleys, a local building company. Unlike most churches, it has no tower to mark its position, and few people passing through Astwood Bank will even realise that there is a church there (see photograph A163005, below).

Needles are still made in the Redditch area by Entaco (English Needle & Tackle Company) at Studley, which produces millions of needles every week. Needles are made for a huge variety of purposes, ranging from hundreds of categories of domestic and hand sewing needles, and thousands of types of medical and surgical needles, fishing hooks and tattooing needles, as well as a wide selection of needles for industrial purposes, from saddle-making and upholstery to the requirements of the space age.

ASTWOOD BANK, THE PARISH CHURCH c1965 A163005

THE ABBEY STADIUM SPORTS GROUND c1965 R84060

SPORTING REDDITCH

The roots of Redditch United FC can be traced back to at least 1891. At that time the club, known as Redditch Town, played in the Birmingham Combination League. One of the highlights of the club's history occurred in the early 1970s, when it reached the first round proper of the FA Cup. Redditch United were drawn against Peterborough United, and took them to a replay before eventually losing.

Redditch Arrows American Football Club have had a very successful history. Between 1988 and 2004 they were winners or runners up in at least 15 competitions.

Redditch was the home town of a 19th-century English bare-knuckle boxing champion, Tom Paddock, known as the Redditch Needlepointer. He was born in the town in 1824, and began his career in 1844. Ten years later he won the English heavyweight title when he beat William Thompson to claim the championship. Bare-knuckle fighting was a brutal and illegal business. Paddock's title fight lasted for 49 rounds, taking more than an hour.

Redditch was important in the development of the sport of angling. The town was a major centre for needle-making in the 17th and 18th centuries, and from this an industry in fishing hooks developed, to satisfy the demand for good quality equipment in the flourishing sport during the 1700s. By 1780, the hooks were in wide spread use and were being exported to America.

QUIZ QUESTIONS

Answers on page 48.

1. How did Redditch get its name?

2. Who is the figure on the fountain on Church Green supposed to represent? (See photograph R84016x, opposite)

3. A Redditch printing company, B B Print Digital Ltd, made the headlines a few years ago when it produced a successful novelty calendar featuring ... what?

4. How did Redditch help to win the Battle of Britain of the Second World War?

5. With which two towns is Redditch twinned?

6. Local place-names around Redditch often end in -ley (for instance Batchley, Beoley, Bordesley, Bridley, Ipsley and Studley) - what does -ley mean?

7. What were once 'Built Like a Gun' in Redditch?

8. What is the link between Redditch and the rock band Led Zeppelin?

9. Which Redditch-born actor starred in the 2005 BBC adaptation of Charles Dickens's 'Bleak House'?

10. What is the link between Redditch and the space shuttle Columbia?

THE FOUNTAIN, CHURCH GREEN
c1950 R84016x

RECIPE

ONION GRAVY

This recipe, using Worcestershire Sauce, is a reminder of the days when special excursion trains ran from Redditch to the Birmingham Onion Fair. Onion gravy is particularly good served with sausages or faggots.

Ingredients

2 tablespoonfuls vegetable oil

1 large onion, halved then sliced

1 tablespoonful plain flour

360ml/12fl oz good stock

1 teaspoonful chopped mixed herbs, fresh or dried

1 teaspoonful Worcestershire Sauce

Heat the oil in a medium sized saucepan. Add the onions and sauté for about 10 minutes, until brown. Sprinkle the flour over the onions and continue to cook, stirring gently, for 2-3 minutes. Gradually add the stock, herbs and Worcestershire Sauce and continue to cook until thickened, stirring all the time. Partially cover and cook for a further 10-15 minutes to allow the flavours to develop, stirring from time to time.

THE PARADE, CHURCH GREEN WEST
c1950 R84010

THE GARDEN OF REMEMBRANCE c1960 R84047

RECIPE

ST STEPHEN'S DAY PIE

The church on Church Green at Redditch is dedicated to St Stephen. St Stephen's Day is 26 December, better known as Boxing Day. This recipe is a good way of using up left-over Christmas turkey and ham, but can also be made with chicken.

Ingredients
60g/2oz butter
1 large onion, finely chopped
300ml/10fl oz double cream
100ml/3½fl oz chicken or turkey stock
450g/1lb mushrooms, sliced
1 tablespoonful chopped tarragon or marjoram
675g/1lb 5oz cooked turkey and ham, cut into chunks
1.2kg/2½lb potatoes
A small knob of butter for cooking the mushrooms
1 egg yolk
3 tablespoonfuls milk
Salt and freshly ground black pepper

To make the mashed potato: Place the potatoes in a saucepan of boiling water and cook until soft. When cooked, drain the potatoes, return them to the saucepan and mash roughly. Add 30g/1oz of the butter, egg yolk and milk, and mash to a thick paste. Season to taste with salt and freshly ground black pepper.

Whilst the potatoes are cooking: Melt the remaining 30g/1oz of butter in a large saucepan, and add the chopped onion. Cook on a gentle heat for about 10 minutes, until the onions are completely soft. Season with salt and freshly ground black pepper. Add the cream and stock, bring to the boil and simmer for a few minutes to thicken, then put aside. Melt the extra knob of butter in a separate pan and cook the mushrooms for a few minutes until soft. Add the tarragon or marjoram, and season to taste. Add the chunks of meat and cooked mushrooms to the cream mixture and stir well. Pour the meat and cream mixture into a shallow gratin dish.

When the mashed potato has been prepared, use it to top the meat and cream mixture in the gratin dish. Cook in a pre-heated oven for 20-30 minutes (180 degrees C/360 degrees F/Gas Mark 4), until the potato topping is golden brown.

MARKET PLACE c1955 R84027

HUINS SHOES

QUIZ ANSWERS

1. The first recorded mention of a settlement in the Redditch area was in 1248, when the name was Rededitch, or Red-dyche. It is said to have taken its name from Batchley Brook, which runs through a layer of water-staining red marl.

2. The figure on the fountain on Church Green is believed to represent Temperance.

3. The company decided to produce a novelty calendar featuring 12 of the many roundabouts in the confusing traffic system for which Redditch is famous. The idea proved so successful that the company has produced similar calendars for other towns - see www.roundaboutsofbritain.com

4. According to local historians Alan Foxall and Ray Saunders in their fascinating book 'Redditch At War', the efficient production of pistons and propellers in the town by High Duty Alloys Ltd was a major contributor to the swift expansion of the RAF during the Second World War, and the subsequent success of the Battle of Britain.

5. Redditch is twinned with Auxerre in France and Mtwara in Tanzania.

6. The ending of -ley in a place-name indicates that these were originally Saxon settlements, based on clearings in the Forest of Feckenham (another Saxon name), probably made from the 6th century onwards.

7. Royal Enfield motorcycles. The Royal Enfield Manufacturing Company was an important business in Redditch in the 19th and 20th centuries. The original company, known as the Eadie Manufacturing Company, won a contract with the Royal Small Arms factory in Enfield, Middlesex, to supply precision parts for Enfield rifles. When the company moved into manufacturing motorcycles, this inspired both the name for the company and its marketing slogan, 'Built Like a Gun, Goes Like a Bullet'. The manufacture of Royal Enfield motorcycles in England ceased in 1970 (when operations were moved to India), but some of the factory buildings still stand on the Enfield Industrial Estate.

8. John Bonham, the drummer in the rock band Led Zeppelin, was born in Redditch in 1948. Led Zeppelin were one of the most popular bands in the world from the late 1960s to 1980, when they effectively disbanded following Bonham's death. At a council meeting in 2003, Councillor Phil Mould said that 'John Bonham' should be included in the list of possible names for future roads in Redditch.

9. Charles Dance, who played the evil lawyer Mr Tulkinghorn in 'Bleak House', was born in Redditch in 1946.

10. Redditch needles were used to attach heat-resistant barrier tiles to the space shuttle Columbia.

Did You Know?
REDDITCH
A MISCELLANY

HEPWORTHS.

FRANCIS FRITH

PIONEER VICTORIAN PHOTOGRAPHER

Francis Frith, founder of the world-famous photographic archive, was a complex and multi-talented man. A devout Quaker and a highly successful Victorian businessman, he was philosophical by nature and pioneering in outlook. By 1855 he had already established a wholesale grocery business in Liverpool, and sold it for the astonishing sum of £200,000, which is the equivalent today of over £15,000,000. Now in his thirties, and captivated by the new science of photography, Frith set out on a series of pioneering journeys up the Nile and to the Near East.

INTRIGUE AND EXPLORATION

He was the first photographer to venture beyond the sixth cataract of the Nile. Africa was still the mysterious 'Dark Continent', and Stanley and Livingstone's historic meeting was a decade into the future. The conditions for picture taking confound belief. He laboured for hours in his wicker dark-room in the sweltering heat of the desert, while the volatile chemicals fizzed dangerously in their trays. Back in London he exhibited his photographs and was 'rapturously cheered' by members of the Royal Society. His reputation as a photographer was made overnight.

VENTURE OF A LIFE-TIME

By the 1870s the railways had threaded their way across the country, and Bank Holidays and half-day Saturdays had been made obligatory by Act of Parliament. All of a sudden the working man and his family were able to enjoy days out, take holidays, and see a little more of the world.

With typical business acumen, Francis Frith foresaw that these new tourists would enjoy having souvenirs to commemorate their days out. For the next thirty years he travelled the country by train and by pony and trap, producing fine photographs of seaside resorts and beauty spots that were keenly bought by millions of Victorians. These prints were painstakingly pasted into family albums and pored over during the dark nights of winter, rekindling precious memories of summer excursions. Frith's studio was soon supplying retail shops all over the country, and by 1890 F Frith & Co had become the greatest specialist photographic publishing company in the world, with over 2,000 sales outlets, and pioneered the picture postcard.

FRANCIS FRITH'S LEGACY

Francis Frith had died in 1898 at his villa in Cannes, his great project still growing. By 1970 the archive he created contained over a third of a million pictures showing 7,000 British towns and villages.

Frith's legacy to us today is of immense significance and value, for the magnificent archive of evocative photographs he created provides a unique record of change in the cities, towns and villages throughout Britain over a century and more. Frith and his fellow studio photographers revisited locations many times down the years to update their views, compiling for us an enthralling and colourful pageant of British life and character.

We are fortunate that Frith was dedicated to recording the minutiae of everyday life. For it is this sheer wealth of visual data, the painstaking chronicle of changes in dress, transport, street layouts, buildings, housing and landscape that captivates us so much today, offering us a powerful link with the past and with the lives of our ancestors.

Computers have now made it possible for Frith's many thousands of images to be accessed almost instantly. The archive offers every one of us an opportunity to examine the places where we and our families have lived and worked down the years. Its images, depicting our shared past, are now bringing pleasure and enlightenment to millions around the world a century and more after his death.

For further information visit: www.francisfrith.com

INTERIOR DECORATION

Frith's photographs can be seen framed and as giant wall murals in thousands of pubs, restaurants, hotels, banks, retail stores and other public buildings throughout Britain. These provide interesting and attractive décor, generating strong local interest and acting as a powerful reminder of gentler days in our increasingly busy and frenetic world.

FRITH PRODUCTS

All Frith photographs are available as prints and posters in a variety of different sizes and styles. In the UK we also offer a range of other gift and stationery products illustrated with Frith photographs, although many of these are not available for delivery outside the UK – see our web site for more information on the products available for delivery in your country.

THE INTERNET

Over 100,000 photographs of Britain can be viewed and purchased on the Frith web site. The web site also includes memories and reminiscences contributed by our customers, who have personal knowledge of localities and of the people and properties depicted in Frith photographs. If you wish to learn more about a specific town or village you may find these reminiscences fascinating to browse. Why not add your own comments if you think they would be of interest to others? See **www.francisfrith.com**

PLEASE HELP US BRING FRITH'S PHOTOGRAPHS TO LIFE

Our authors do their best to recount the history of the places they write about. They give insights into how particular towns and villages developed, they describe the architecture of streets and buildings, and they discuss the lives of famous people who lived there. But however knowledgeable our authors are, the story they tell is necessarily incomplete.

Frith's photographs are so much more than plain historical documents. They are living proofs of the flow of human life down the generations. They show real people at real moments in history; and each of those people is the son or daughter of someone, the brother or sister, aunt or uncle, grandfather or grandmother of someone else. All of them lived, worked and played in the streets depicted in Frith's photographs.

We would be grateful if you would give us your insights into the places shown in our photographs: the streets and buildings, the shops, businesses and industries. Post your memories of life in those streets on the Frith website: what it was like growing up there, who ran the local shop and what shopping was like years ago; if your workplace is shown tell us about your working day and what the building is used for now. Read other visitors' memories and reconnect with your shared local history and heritage. With your help more and more Frith photographs can be brought to life, and vital memories preserved for posterity, and for the benefit of historians in the future.

Wherever possible, we will try to include some of your comments in future editions of our books. Moreover, if you spot errors in dates, titles or other facts, please let us know, because our archive records are not always completely accurate—they rely on 140 years of human endeavour and hand-compiled records. You can email us using the contact form on the website.

Thank you!

For further information, trade, or author enquiries please contact us at the address below:

The Francis Frith Collection, Frith's Barn, Teffont, Salisbury, Wiltshire, England SP3 5QP.
Tel: +44 (0)1722 716 376 Fax: +44 (0)1722 716 881
e-mail: sales@francisfrith.co.uk **www.francisfrith.com**